Your will

Be done

30DAY DEVOTIONS

CORINA MAUSALI

"Scripture quotations taken from the Amplified® Bible (AMP), Copyright © 2015 by The Lockman Foundation Used by permission. www.Lockman.org"

Edited by Traneisha Jones with T Jones Media in Chicago, Illinois.

Cover design by Elisha Scott with Elisha Scott Studio in Cincinnati, Ohio.

Dedication

For those who are reading this, may it bless you as much as it has blessed me to write this and put it together. My prayer is that this book will help encourage, uplift, heal, deliver and bring peace and comfort to you.

Acknowledgement

This book was developed as a result of reading the Word of God and spending time with Him, in His presence. I include a special thanks to God for everything He has done, is doing and continues to do in my life. He has brought me through so much and it's because of Him and the love He has given me, that I can write and complete this book.

I give thanks to my father Pouono Mausali, who showed my sisters and I, the same love God has for His children. He was a great provider, encourager, protector, counselor and friend with a funny sense of humor. He told me I could do anything I put my mind to. I miss him very much, but I know I will see him again. If you could see me now Daddy and the work God continues to do in me, I know you would be so proud!

Thank you, Mommy! Yes, I still call her that. Thank you Mrs. Fiaaliali Mausali for being my opposite and sharpening me every chance you get. Your prayer meetings helped me grow in my prayer life.

To my husband, Eric K Payne, I thank you for impelling me to be the best you know I can be, even when I don't want to go the extra mile. I thank you for pushing me closer to God. You remind me every day that I am still in the making to be what God needs me to be.

To my daughters, Unity and Uriah, who God has blessed me with. I know I have been some kind of wonderful to you both throughout the years. I want to ask you both for forgiveness of any wrong I have done in raising you two. I am not perfect but know I love you two very much and that God loves you both so much more. He offers more than I or this world can give. Hold close to Him and never let Him go.

I'd also like to thank my sister Sonya Mausali, who is not only my biological sister but also my sister in Christ Jesus. You have been such a blessing to me on this journey. We have learned and are still learning so much from each other and enjoying our walk with God and the people and places He sets in our paths. Thank you for allowing me to share with you my testimonies, revelations and experiences.

Lots of love to my other sisters Amy, Diana, Patsy and Marcia (who is no longer here with us but is present with the Lord) for being supportive in your own ways, thank you!

To Sophia Ruffin, thank you for letting God use you in such a powerful way and for sharing such vital information to help others in the Body to do what we took so long to do without your push. I really love your rawness and realness. You are the Real, Raw, Rough-In (Ruffin) people up Coach. I love you and thank you for your words of encouragement and the love you have for the people of God. You Rock!

Thank you Traneisha Jones for being a blessing in editing and putting the final touches needed to make this book complete.

Last and not least, a big huge thank you to Elisha Scott with Elisha Scott Studio for the awesome book cover. You came in at a short notice and completed the project before the deadline. I am forever grateful!

DAY ONE

Isaiah 41:10 (AMP)

'Do not fear [anything], for I am with you;
Do not be afraid, for I am your God.
I will strengthen you, be assured I will help you;
I will certainly take hold of you with My righteous
right hand [a hand of justice, of power, of victory, of
salvation].'

Message:

My child, do not be afraid of anything that may come
your way spiritually, mentally or physically for I AM
with you. I AM the help and confidence you need. I
will strengthen you and lift you up in My hands which
I have wonderfully and beautifully created you with.
Trust I AM here for you. I will never leave you nor
forsake you. You are mine and nothing can take you
from the palms of My hands unless you choose to
walk away from Me.

Prayer:

Father in the name Jesus, I thank You for holding me
close. Thank you for reminding me that You are here

with me. Help me Lord to stay close to You, and when it seems like I am wandering off, place Your heavenly angel before me to bring me back to You. When I'm down and feeling weak, let me feel Your warm embrace all around so I know that You are there. In Jesus' mighty name, Amen.

DAY TWO

1 John 3:16-18 (AMP)

By this we know [and have come to understand the depth and essence of His precious] love: that He [willingly] laid down His life for us [because He loved us]. And we ought to lay down our lives for the believers. But whoever has the world's goods (adequate resources), and sees his brother in need, but has no compassion for him, how does the love of God live in him? Little children (believers, dear ones), let us not love [merely in theory] with word or with tongue [giving lip service to compassion], but in action and in truth [in practice and in sincerity, because practical acts of love are more than words].

Message:

Do you understand how deep My love is for you? It is so deep that I laid down My life so I could live within you because I crave to be close to you. The same love I displayed, should be the same love all should demonstrate; being there for one another and helping those who are in need with compassion of understanding with where they are in that moment in time. Let's mean and do what we say. Actions speak louder than words. We need to show love. Therefore, I AM love and so are you. Love enough to be a blessing to someone else.

Prayer:

Father God, I thank You for the understanding to know the love You have for us all. For You gave Your only begotten Son to die on the cross and raised Him up three days later, so we could have this opportunity to come before You and be cleansed from our sins. Lord may You use me in such a way to help those in need. In everything I do, let it be done as if being done unto You. Let Your light shine through me for all to see like a light house shining its light for the lost to find their way back home. Create in me a love so pure that everything I touch and everything I do will be done with gladness and joy in the mighty name of Jesus, Amen.

DAY THREE

Psalm 73:26 (AMP)

My flesh and my heart may fail, But God is the rock and strength of my heart and my portion forever.

Message:

No matter how much you want to give up because someone has hurt you or has broken your heart, know that I AM your rock who withstands time and will never fail you. I AM the God of eternity. Come to Me for I will give you rest. I AM the piece of the puzzle that can and will make your heart whole and complete.

Prayer:

Father in the name of Jesus, I thank you for the strength You give me to fight through this pain and hurt. I know You will never fail me. Lord I ask for You to strengthen my faith and trust that You will bring me through it even when I don't see it happening right away. Help me to be patient in the process of what You are doing and to hold close to You. In Jesus' mighty name, Amen.

DAY FOUR

1 Peter 5:10 (AMP)

After you have suffered for a little while, the God of all grace [who imparts His blessing and favor], who called you to His own eternal glory in Christ, will Himself complete, confirm, strengthen, and establish you [making you what you ought to be].

Message:

When you feel like you are suffering, it will only be for a little while because you are in this world, but not of it. Remember I have called you to be Mine and I will give you the strength you need to complete the journey or whatever assignment I have instructed for you to do. You have My blessings and favor over your life and the confirmation is where I AM taking you and what I AM creating you to be.

Prayer:

Father in the name of Jesus, I pray for the endurance in this time of suffering. I know this is for a short season and I believe this is something I may be going through to get me ready for where You are taking me next. Help me Lord to keep my eyes fixated on You. In Jesus' name, Amen.

DAY FIVE

1 Corinthians 15:58 (AMP)

Therefore, my beloved brothers and sisters, be steadfast, immovable, always excelling in the work of the Lord [always doing your best and doing more than is needed], being continually aware that your labor [even to the point of exhaustion] in the Lord is not futile nor wasted [it is never without purpose].

Message:

My children, be steady, anchored, going above and beyond doing the footwork for the Kingdom of Heaven. At the same time know that what you are doing is never a waste of time. Even when you're tired, continue to push with the strength I have given you, because everything you have done up until this point has a purpose bigger than anyone can imagine. It would be such an advantage for the Kingdom of Heaven if each one, can teach one to reach one.

Prayer:

Lord I come before You and ask for Your spiritual wisdom, knowledge and understanding to do what it is that You have called me to do for Your people and Kingdom. Thank You Lord for You are the foundation that my house is built on. With You I can weather any storm or flood that may come against me. You taught me to speak things into existence and like Jesus when He spoke to the storm to be still, I speak to the storm to be still in the name of Jesus. Father God, You are my Strongtower and I run to You and I am strengthened. Help me to continue to hold fast to Your Word of life and give You all the glory and honor for I do not run this race hopeless but for Your purpose, in Jesus' mighty name, Amen.

DAY SIX

James 5:16 (AMP)

Therefore, confess your sins to one another [your false steps, your offenses], and pray for one another, that you may be healed and restored. The heartfelt and persistent prayer of a righteous man (believer) can accomplish much [when put into action and made effective by God-it is dynamic and can have tremendous power].

Message:

For you to be healed and restored from the pain or hurt, you must first confess your sins and the sins of those committed against you. I will forgive you and those who hurt you if you just ask, then you must repent and turn away from those sins. The pain and hurt is the reason for your sickness or whatever abnormality is taking place in your health. I search the heart of those who are genuine about the prayer they are praying. If you believe in Me and all that I AM and follow these simple steps, each sin you prayed about will be heard and answered. But you must do your part in never going back to it, and instead do something new and beneficial for you spiritually, mentally and physically. You will then see and understand the power I have given you to be healed.

Prayer:

Father in the name of Jesus, I ask you to forgive me for the sins I have committed knowingly and unknowingly and forgive those who have sinned against me. Lord I repent of my sins and turn away from it. I believe You are the Only True Living God who can heal and make me whole. There are some days I feel are harder than others and I pray Holy Spirit for the remembrance of God's Word to help me through them and to know that this too shall pass and that I can do all things in Christ Jesus who strengthens me, in Jesus' mighty name, Amen.

DAY SEVEN

Psalm 46:1-2 (AMP)

God is our refuge and strength [mighty and impenetrable], A very present and well proved help in trouble. Therefore, we will not fear, though the earth should change and though the mountains be shaken and slip into the heart of the seas...

Message:

Come to Me and I will shelter and protect you from whatever you may be going through. I AM not only the God in the Holy Bible, but I AM also the God of today, tomorrow, yesterday and forever. I AM everywhere at the same time. I AM where you are because I AM with you as I AM with Him. You don't need to fear anything regardless of what takes place in your life. It may look like your world is being turned upside down or things are not going your way, but know that with Me it will be placed right side up and will go the way I planned it to go.

Prayer:

Lord help me to keep my eyes on you and not my situation, for you are the God of everything, knowing and seeing everything. You knew me before I was even created in my mother's womb. Your Word tells me not to fear anything for You are with me and will strengthen me. Thank You Lord that You know the plans and thoughts You have for me, plans for peace and wellbeing and not for disaster or evil, to give me a future and hope, in Jesus' mighty name, Amen.

DAY EIGHT

1 Timothy 4:12 (AMP)

Let no one look down on [you because of] your youth, but be an example and set a pattern for the believers in speech, in conduct, in love, in faith, and in [moral] purity.

Message:

Some people will look down on you because of your age or because you have been with Me for less years than they have. Don't let it get to you because I am pouring Myself into those who are seeking Me with all their mind, heart and soul. You have the mind of

Christ Jesus and are filled with My love and compassion. I have given you the Words to speak to them in love and show them the love I have shown you through My Son Jesus' demonstration on the cross. Be watchful and mindful for there are people watching you; and the choices and moves you make, can bring someone to Me or keep them from Me. Continue to carefully show yourself approved unto Me, unashamed and rightly handling My Word and Truth because you are the child of the Most High God.

Prayer:

Father in the name of Jesus, I ask you to open my heart and fill it with Your love so that I can love on those who are hurting. Let me see what You see and hear what You hear when I am placed in front of them. May the Holy Spirit speak through me with such love that it pierces them right where it hurts so that they run into Your arms and seek Your face like never before. Guide my steps to what is right and away from what is wrong. For You are a lamp to my feet and a light to my path. Let them see You in me, in Jesus' name, Amen.

DAY NINE

Philippians 4:19 (AMP)

And my God will liberally supply (fill until full) your every need according to His riches in glory in Christ Jesus.

Message:

I will generously give you all you need according to My riches in the Kingdom of Heaven. You can have heaven here on earth but you need to tap into the heavenly realm to bring it into the natural by spending more time with Me. I can show you the mysteries I have hidden for only those who are willing and open to receive and believe in Me.

Prayer:

Thank you Lord for being my provider. You supply my every need. There may be things I want, but You know what is best for me. Thank You Father for wanting to share with me Your hidden mysteries and for opening the doors for my eyes to see what it is You need me to see. Remind me Lord to be thankful for all that You do, all that You have done and all that You continue to do in my life, in Jesus' mighty name, Amen.

DAY TEN

John 16:33 (AMP)

I have told you these things, so that in Me you may have [perfect] peace. In the world you have tribulation and distress and suffering, but be courageous [be confident, be undaunted, be filled with joy]; I have overcome the world." [My conquest is accomplished, My victory abiding.]

Message:

I have given you My peace that surpasses all understanding. This peace I give to you, but not to the world. In this world you will go through trials, stress, and suffering but know that I AM with you and live in you. I have conquered this world and I have given you the power and authority to do the same. Be bold, strong, levelheaded and filled with joy because you can defeat this world by fighting the good fight and walking it out.

Prayer:

Heavenly Father, thank You for Your peace and for allowing me to rest in You knowing that I am not in this alone and that You have given me the keys and tools I need to fight this battle. You are the King of kings and Lord of lords, and you have given me the power and authority to trample on the heads of snakes and scorpions. Thank You Lord for I am Your righteousness standing on the Rock. In Jesus' mighty name, Amen.

DAY ELEVEN

Psalm 34:19 (AMP)

Many hardships and perplexing circumstances confront the righteous, But the Lord rescues him from them all.

Message:

You will go through some rough times and be thrown off balance but know I AM here for you. Trust in Me and lean not unto your own understanding, but in all your ways and in everything you do, acknowledge Me and I will direct your paths.

Father I thank You for directing my paths so I don't have to go through as much hardship as I would without You. I understand some things will happen, but I know You are in control. Thank You Lord for keeping me steady and under the shadow of Your wings of protection, in Jesus' mighty name, Amen.

DAY TWELVE

Isaiah 49:15-16 (AMP)

[The Lord answered] "Can a woman forget her nursing child and have no compassion on the son of her womb? Even these may forget, but I will not forget you. Indeed, I have inscribed [a picture of] you on the palms of My hands; Your city walls [Zion] are continually before Me.

Message:

My love for you is greater than the love a mother has for her child. She can get caught up with the things of this world and forget her child. But I have made a commitment and promise to you that I will be there for you. I AM not a man that I should lie and will not go back on My Word. I will keep you wherever you go until I have done what I have promised.

Prayer:

Father God I thank You for Your unconditional love You have for me. I am holding onto Your promise and standing on Your every Word. I believe You are who You say You are, and wherever I go You are there, for You are not a promise breaker but a promise maker. Thank You for keeping me not only in the palms of Your hands but also on Your mind constantly, in Jesus' mighty name, Amen.

DAY THIRTEEN

Proverbs 21:21 (AMP)

He who earnestly seeks righteousness and loyalty; finds life, righteousness and honor.

Message:

Whoever seriously desires truth and faith will find life, honor and favor.

Prayer:

Lord I seek You with all my heart, mind and soul. I want what you have for me. You say that I am Your righteousness and You will give me the desires of my heart. I ask You to fill me up with more of You and empty me of anything and everything that is not of You. Let me be the spitting image of Your Righteousness, walking in Your Truth. In Jesus' mighty name, Amen.

DAY FOURTEEN

1 Peter 1:8-9 (AMP)

Though you have not seen Him, you love Him; and though you do not even see Him now, you believe and trust in Him and you greatly rejoice and delight with inexpressible and glorious joy, receiving as the result [the outcome, the consummation] of your faith, the salvation of your souls.

Message:

You have not seen Me, yet you love Me and know I exist. Because of your belief, you still trust in Me that the happiness and joy you are going through is so great it is indescribable.

Prayer:

My Lord, I may not see You naturally but I know and trust You exist in everything around me. For You are the Creator of all things great and small. My heart rejoices in all that You do. I thank You for Your goodness and mercy that shall follow me all the days of my life, in Jesus' mighty name, Amen.

DAY FIFTEEN

Isaiah 40:28-31 (AMP)

Do you not know? Have you not heard? The Everlasting God, the Lord, the Creator of the ends of the earth does not become weary; There is no searching of His understanding. He gives strength to the weary, and to him who has no might He increases power. Even youths grow weary and tired, and vigorous young men stumble badly. But those who wait for the Lord [who expect, look for, and hope in

Him] will gain new strength and renew their power; They will lift up their wings [and rise up close to God like eagles [rising toward the sun]; They will run and not become weary, they will walk and not grow tired.

Message:

I AM God the Creator of all heaven and earth and all things great and small. My power and strength is so great I have enough to give to all who are in need and seeking Me desperately. You must wait patiently and diligently, and seek Me in the process. By doing this and remaining focused, you will not even notice that I AM carrying you across and walking you through it. I AM your second wind.

Prayer:

Thank You Lord for Your power that gives me the patience and strength to endure, defeat and triumph over the things this world brings. You have given me the power to be victorious over everything. Thank You Lord for showing me to rely only on You because there is nothing impossible You can't do. You are the Unchangeable and Living God, and You are more than enough for me. Thank You Lord in Jesus' mighty name, Amen.

DAY SIXTEEN

Jeremiah 17:14 (AMP)

Heal mc, O Lord, and I will be healed; Save me and I will be saved, for You are my praise.

Message:

Praise Me for being the Healer of all healers and the only Saviour who can save.

Prayer:

Father God I give You all the glory, honor and praise. You have healed me of my infirmities and have saved me from not only this world but from myself. Thank You Lord for giving me another chance to making things right in Your eyes. For I am not here to please man, but to serve as You have sent Your Son in the world to serve. In Jesus' mighty name, Amen.

DAY SEVENTEEN

1 Corinthians 13:3 (AMP)

If I give all my possessions to feed the poor, and if I surrender my body to be burned, but do not have love, it does me no good at all.

Message:

What good is it if you give all your things away to help the poor and give yourself up to the things that will burn you without any love? There is no purpose in it. I search the intentions of the hearts. I AM looking for lovers who will out work the workers. Lovers will outlast and endure to the end because they don't look at the assignment, they do the assignment. With joy and such gladness, it does not become work to them but fellowship and communion unto Me.

Prayer:

Father You are Love. You show Your love for all to see. I pray You will break my heart for what breaks Yours. Let Your love flow within my veins. May I continue to be the sweet aroma of Jesus Christ to You among those who are being saved and among those who are perishing but to the other a vital fragrance, living and fresh, in Jesus' mighty name, Amen.

DAY EIGHTEEN

1 Thessalonians 4:13-14 (AMP)

Now we do not want you to be uninformed, believers, about those who are asleep [in death], so that you will not grieve [for them] as the others do who have no hope [beyond this present life]. For if we believe that Jesus died and rose again [as in fact He did], even so God [in this same way – by raising them from the dead] will bring with Him those [believers] who have fallen asleep in Jesus.

Message:

For those who believed in Me and are no longer physically here, they are only resting until I come back. Don't cry like you will never see them again unless you don't know where they're going. If they were believers in Me before leaving this world I will raise them like I raised My Son, upon My return to gather the rest of the true believers and followers. I AM coming soon. Where we are going there will be no more tears, pain, mourning or death for the old order of things has passed away and in Me and through Me all things will be and are created new.

Prayer:

Father God I thank You for Your assurance and hope You have placed in me. I know my loved ones who have gone before me are no longer suffering and are just resting until we are all called up into the air with You. Thank You for wiping away my tears and for keeping them in a bottle in remembrance to You of my pain and sorrow I was going through. But because I am more than a conqueror in You, I am confident You are by my side and believe what You say in Jesus' name, Amen.

DAY NINETEEN

Exodus 15:26 (AMP)

And said, "If you diligently heed the voice of the Lord your God and do what is right in His sight, give ear to His commandments and keep all His statutes, I will put none of the diseases on you which I have brought on the Egyptians. For I am the Lord who heals you."

Message:

If you follow My instructions from the Holy Bible and listen to My Word, you can prevent getting most of the diseases out there in this world. My Word explains how you can be healed and stay healed spiritually, mentally and physically. If My people who are called by My name, would humble themselves, and pray, and seek My face and turn from their wicked ways; then will I hear from heaven, and will forgive their sin, and will heal their land.

Prayer:

Lord I ask You for forgiveness from anything and everything I, my parents, and ancestors going back all the way to my forefathers have done that was contrary to Your Word. I also pray that You forgive all of us in this nation for turning our backs on You and Your commandments. Father I bow before you on my face in humility and pray You release Your supernatural healing over us all and this land. I pray for Your supernatural cleansing not only in us, but also over everything that man has touched and made impure that You created good. Help us Lord to be obedient in hearing You and drowning out the distractions of this world, in Jesus' mighty name, Amen.

DAY TWENTY

Romans 8:18-21 (AMP)

For I consider [from the standpoint of faith] that the sufferings of the present life are not worthy to be compared with the glory that is about to be revealed to us and in us! For [even the whole] creations [all nature] waits eagerly for the children of God to be revealed. For the creation was subjected to frustration and futility not willingly [because of some intentional fault on its part], but by the will of Him who subjected it, in hope that the creation itself will also be freed from its bondage to decay [and gain entrance] into the glorious freedom of the children of God.

Message:

Due to the sin of man, all of My creation will suffer but there is hope in Me that something good will come out of this. Trials will come but it's nothing compare to what You know I AM doing on your behalf. Suffering is part of the human condition but remember the faith and strength I have given you. During these times you will see how I AM causing it to turn around and work together for your good.

Prayer:

Father, You make me stronger and I thank You for being my hope through my seasons of trials. You are my Strongtower and in You I will hide. In Your Word I am reminded of who I am and the power I have been given. Thank You, Jesus, for turning things around for my good. Thank You for allowing me to go through it so You can continue to build me up and strengthen me for the next battle, in Jesus' mighty name, Amen.

DAY TWENTY-ONE

Leviticus 19:17-18 (AMP)

You shall not hate your brother in your heart; you may most certainly rebuke your neighbor, but shall not incur sin because of him. You shall not take revenge nor bear any grudge against the sons of your people, but you shall love your neighbor (acquaintance, associate, companion) as yourself; I AM the Lord.

Message:

It is okay to be angry but acting or holding on to it will only cause you to be sick. Discuss your issues amongst each other with an open heart of understanding and give one another the opportunity to be heard without interrupting. This will and can help you be at peace not only with each other, but also with yourself.

Prayer:

Father God You are in control and I ask that You control my mind. Lord help me to have Your understanding and an open heart to all those You place in front of me that can be difficult to deal with. Father help me to be quick to listen and forgive, and slow to speak and be angry. Thank You Lord for making it right, in Jesus' name, Amen.

DAY TWENTY-TWO

Roman 13:8 (AMP)

Owe nothing to anyone except to love and seek the best for one another; for he who [unselfishly] loves his neighbor has fulfilled the [essence of the] law [relating to one's fellowman].

Message:

To love your neighbor is to love anyone who comes across your path, not just the person who lives next door. Do what you can to help others, and you will not have to live with the feeling that you could've done something, but neglected to when you had the opportunity to do so. This is the love I AM talking about when I say you should love your neighbor as yourself.

Prayer:

Lord I pray that when I look at anyone, I will see You. By seeing You, I see myself. I am a reflection of You, Your Word and Your Truth. I pray Your love will radiate through me everywhere I step foot. Lord help me to see and seize the opportunities You place before me to display and show Your love. Make me available to help where You need me in Jesus' mighty name, Amen.

DAY TWENTY-THREE

1 Corinthians 16:13 (AMP)

Be on guard; stand firm in your faith [in God, respecting His precepts and keeping your doctrine sound]. Act like [mature] men and be courageous; be strong.

Message:

Be watchful and stand strong in your faith in Me, keeping My Word. Be fearless and in having all the power to stand.

Prayer:

Father I thank You for the power You have given me over all the power of the enemy. Because of Your victory, I am no longer afraid. I have defeated the spirit of fear and it pleases You to give me the keys to Your Kingdom. Thank You Lord for the courage to do all I can to stand. Thank You Jesus for being the bridge for me to cross over in Your mighty and precious name, Amen.

DAY TWENTY-FOUR

Hebrews 10:24-25 (AMP)

And let us consider [thoughtfully] how we may encourage one another to love and to do good deeds, not forsaking our meeting together [as believers for worship and instruction], as is the habit of some, but encouraging one another; and all the more [faithfully] as you see the day [of Christ's return] approaching.

Message:

As brothers and sisters in My Son Jesus Christ, gather together to break bread. As it is written, man shall not live by bread alone but by every Word that proceeds from My mouth. Support each other with one mind, one heart and one soul. Be the iron that sharpens iron. Be accountable and responsible for each other and motivate one another on this journey as the day of My Son's return draws near.

Prayer:

Father in the name Jesus, thank You for giving us the opportunity to gather in worship and fellowship. For we know there are others in countries that are being persecuted, murdered, and imprisoned for Your sake. You are the Bread of Life and Living Waters flow out like rivers from the bellies of Your people. When we need a refreshing shower, You are our source of power. You are our present help in our time of need. We lift Your name on high. Help us to be there to uplift and motivate each other as well. In Jesus' name, Amen.

DAY TWENTY-FIVE

Deuteronomy 31:8 (AMP)

It is the Lord who goes before you; He will be with
you. He will not fail you or abandon you. Do not fear
or be dismayed."

Message:

I have paved the way for you. I will not let you down
or give you up. I AM with you so do not be afraid.

Prayer:

Thank You Lord for walking before me and making
certain of the path that I should take. Thank You for
never leaving me. It is for this reason that I am not
afraid and trust You wherever I am. In Jesus' name,
Amen.

DAY TWENTY-SIX

1 John 4:4 (AMP)

Little children (believers, dear ones), you are of God and you belong to Him and have [already] overcome them [the agents of the antichrist]; because He who is in you is greater than he (Satan) who is in the world [of sinful mankind].

Message:

My child, you are Mine and you belong to Me. You have already defeated those who are coming against you and My Kingdom because the Holy Spirit from My Son Jesus is living within you, and is more powerful than the enemy and his minions in this world.

Prayer:

Thank You Lord for adopting me into Your family. I am Yours, the child of the Most High God. I have the mind of Jesus Christ and like Him I will preach the gospel of the Kingdom to all nations, heal the sick, cleanse the lepers, raise the dead and cast out demons. No matter the circumstance I will not bow to the enemy for he is a defeated foe and through Jesus I have the victory. I will continue to worship You Lord through it all, for there is none like You. You are my tower of refuge and strength. In Jesus' name, Amen.

DAY TWENTY-SEVEN

2 Corinthians 4:16-18 (AMP)

Therefore, we do not become discouraged [spiritless, disappointed, or afraid]. Though our outer self is [progressively] wasting away, yet our inner self is being [progressively] renewed day by day. For our momentary, light distress [this passing trouble] is producing for us an eternal weight of glory [a fullness] beyond all measure [surpassing all comparisons, a transcendent splendor and an endless blessedness]! So, we look not at the things which are seen, but at the things which are unseen; for the things which are visible are temporal [just brief and fleeting], but the things which are invisible are everlasting and imperishable.

Message:

As time goes by your physique, appearance and things around you will change. This is something that occurs with age, but don't lose hope. Remember you are being transformed by the renewing of your mind constantly in Me every day and you are not to conform to this world; then you will be able to discern what is My pleasing, good and perfect will. What you see in the natural will only last for a moment and will fade, but what is inside of you is everlasting and no one can take that away.

Prayer:

Father God in the name of Jesus, I pray that the Holy Spirit bring to my remembrance my inheritance in the Kingdom of God when it feels like I'm losing hope. For I know my citizenship is in heaven and not of this world. I will continue to look to the hills where my help comes from. Thank You Lord for You began a work in me and You will be faithful to complete it the day You return. In the name of Jesus, Amen.

DAY TWENTY-EIGHT

Proverbs 3:3-4 (AMP)

Do not let mercy and kindness and truth leave you [instead let these qualities define you]; bind them [securely] around your neck, write them on the tablet of your heart. So, find favor and high esteem in the sight of God and man.

Message:

Continue to be faithful, loyal and dedicated in your love towards Me, as I AM towards you. Because you wear these traits like a beautiful garland for all to see and have concerns towards Me, you are praised and pleasing in My eyes. The love you have for Me is so deep, it has changed you forever. Since you chose to be with Me, you have chosen the path that will lead to goodness.

Prayer:

Father, thank You for choosing me and pursuing me before this world began. You chose me for such a time as this, to invest in Your people and to be successful in doing what You have called and assigned me to do for Your Kingdom. Lord, the more I spend time in Your Word, I walk away looking just like You. I love You Lord. I will always remember the love You have for me and how You brought me out of my mess and are faithful to complete Your work in me. In Jesus' name, Amen.

DAY TWENTY-NINE

Matthew 11:28 (AMP)

Come to me, all who are weary and heavily burdened [by religious rituals that provide no peace], and I will give you rest [refreshing your souls with salvation].

Message:

I AM here for you. Let Me give you the break you need and recharge you from the weight of carrying such a difficult load that has made you so weak and tired.

Prayer:

Lord I thank You for Your joy and peace. You make me lie down in green pastures; You lead me beside quiet waters, You restore my soul, and You guide me in the paths of righteousness for Your name's sake. In Your peace, I will both lie down and sleep for You alone, Oh Lord, make me dwell in safety, in the name of Jesus, Amen.

DAY THIRTY

Luke 12:6-7 (AMP)

Are not five sparrows sold for two copper coins? Yet not one of them has [ever] been forgotten in the presence of God. Indeed, the very hairs of your head are all numbered. Do not be afraid; you are far more valuable than many sparrows.

Message:

You My child are very valuable to Me. Just like the sparrows who people probably could care less about, I value you. Every living thing has a spirit that was created by Me. But I have given everyone the free will to choose. For those who have decided to be with Me, you have nothing to fear because My Son Jesus' Holy Spirit is guiding you from within. Although I love all unconditionally, those who are in a relationship with Me, I will guide personally. You have a piece of Me when I created you. What you long for in a relationship is the same yearning I long for in a relationship with you. When you look deep within yourself and open up the doors to your heart, you will find Me.

Prayer:

Lord I have decided to let You come into my life and take over. For I, have tried it on my own for so long and have not found anything that could take the place of this emptiness and void. I need You in my life Lord, to make me whole and brand new in You. This world has nothing to offer me but lies, pain, loss and suffering. Make me free from all these bondages and chains I thought were part of my identity, which everyone and this world has defined me by. Thank You for freeing me of my sins. I thought I had to come to you when I got things straight but the way things are going, it seems like it will take forever if I don't step out now. I am searching for You Lord and I will not stop until I find You. I may have felt that I wasn't worthy, but I now know, how much You love me and yearn for my love. I know how much You value me. I love You Lord because You loved me first. Thank You Jesus for Your light shining on me in this dark world. In Jesus' mighty name, Amen.

www.ingramcontent.com/pod-product-compliance
Lightning Source LLC
Chambersburg PA
CBHW060042040426
42331CB00032B/2168